First published in Great Britain in 2011 by Buster Books,
an imprint of Michael O'Mara Books Limited,
9 Lion Yard, Tremadoc Road, London SW4 7NQ

www.mombooks.com/busterbooks

Text and illustrations copyright © Buster Books 2011
Cover design by Angie Allison
Cover illustrations by Paul Moran

A CIP catalogue record for this book is available from the British Library.

ISBN: 978-1-907151-11-8

2 4 6 8 10 9 7 5 3 1

Papers used by Buster Books are natural, recyclable products
made from wood grown in sustainable forests. The manufacturing processes
conform to the environmental regulations of the country of origin.

Printed and bound in December 2010 by Clays Limited, St Ives plc, Popson Street,
Bungay, Suffolk, NR35 1ED, UK

☆☆☆☆   ☆☆☆☆

CONTENTS

GET READY ... GET SET ... GET SKILLED!

Are you ready to become a super-skilled hero? This book will give you the skills and confidence you need to take on life and win.

Each skill is broken down into simple steps, and there are cool, clear pictures to show you how it's done if you get stuck.

There are six sections to help you find the type of skill you want to master – from chopping an onion in the 'Master-chef' section, to fixing a puncture in 'Do-It-Yourself' or even saving someone's life using 'Emergency Skills'. Read on and you'll discover how amazing it is to be independent.

SKILL SUGGESTION

Look out for boxes like this one in the pages of this book.

Each one contains a top tip or handy hint to help you get the best out of your new-found super-skills.

WARNING

Make sure you read these boxes. They will guarantee that all your skills are performed safely, and will keep you out of danger.

EVERYDAY ESSENTIALS

SKILL 1

CROSS A ROAD

Learning how to cross a road safely is a vital skill. Whether you're in a busy town or faced with a seemingly quiet country lane, here's what to do:

1. Find a safe place to cross. Look for a pelican or zebra crossing nearby. Never cross between parked cars or at the top of a hill.

2. Wait. Never run across, even if a road seems clear. Wait by the kerb to give drivers the chance to see you.

3. Look and listen for cars. Give yourself plenty of time to check out the road in both directions.

4. Wait until there is a big enough gap in the traffic for you to get all the way across the road. If you have to wait in the middle, cross to a traffic island that's wide enough for you to stand on safely.

5. Once the road is clear, walk straight across the road – not diagonally. Keep looking both ways as you go.

SKILL 2

GET BRIGHT WHITE TEETH

Brush your teeth twice a day and follow these simple steps to make sure your teeth stay clean and your breath is minty fresh:

1. Squeeze a pea-sized blob of toothpaste on to your toothbrush.

2. Put one of your favourite songs on the stereo. Brush until the song finishes to make sure you've brushed enough – you should brush your teeth for two minutes, twice a day.

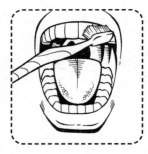

3. Place the toothbrush against your teeth with the bristles at a 45° angle. Move it in small circles over the outside of each tooth.

4. Repeat the motion on the inside surfaces of your teeth.

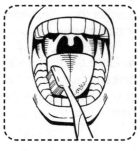

5. To get to the hard-to-reach back teeth, close your mouth slightly around the toothbrush.

6. Brush the tops of your bottom back teeth, and the bottoms of your top back teeth, using a back and forth motion.

7. Brush your tongue to get rid of bacteria and keep your breath smelling fresh.

SKILL 3

BE A HAND WASH HERO

Did you know that it should take you at least 15 seconds to wash your hands properly? Before you eat, after you've been in the garden or been to the loo, follow this bacteria-busting routine to get the cleanest hands around:

1. Wet your hands with warm water and lather up with soap.

2. Rub your palms together in circular motions.

3. Rub the back of each hand with the palm of the other hand, interlacing your fingers as you do so.

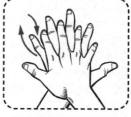

4. Place the pads of your fingers together and pull so that the backs of your fingers are pushing against the palms of your hands. Rub them together.

5. Make a fist with your right hand around your left thumb and rub, then swap hands.

6. Rinse your hands under running water.

SKILL 4

STAY SAFE IN THE SUN

When the sun is shining, you want to be outdoors, at the pool or the local park. To have fun in the sun without burning, remember these simple steps:

1. Don't stay in the sun too long. The sun is strongest from 11 a.m. to 3 p.m., so try and stay indoors at these times. If you are out and about, stay in the shade whenever possible.

2. Wear loose-fitting cotton clothes as well as a hat and sunglasses. Make sure that the lenses have a good UV (ultraviolet) rating to block out harmful rays from the sun.

3. Slap on the sunscreen. Use sunscreen with a sun protection factor (SPF) of at least 30 and put it on ...

SKILL SUGGESTION

Make sure you drink lots of water throughout the day – this will help you stay hydrated and stop you getting sunstroke.

★ ... every bit of your body that's exposed to sun – don't forget your ears and your toes!

★ ... at least 20 minutes before you go out into the sun.

★ ... at least every two hours, and whenever you've been swimming.

BE SAFE ONLINE

**The internet is brilliant, but it can also be dangerous.
If you want to surf safely, follow these tips:**

1. Don't open emails or attachments from people you don't know. They may contain viruses.

2. Keep your passwords and usernames secret so that other people can't access your email accounts.

3. Never, ever give out information such as your home or email address, your real name, age, mobile number or school. If a person or a website asks you for these kind of details,

close the window and end your surf session straightaway.
If in doubt, shut it out.

4. Try and keep your online surfing and real world activities apart. Never meet someone you have contacted online – they might not be who they say they are.

5. If you see anything that makes you feel uncomfortable, tell an adult immediately.

SKILL 6

TIE A TIE

This skill guarantees you'll look smart when you need to. Follow these steps to find out how:

1. If you're wearing your tie with a shirt, put the collar up then put the tie around your neck with its narrow end on your right.

Make sure the wide end of the tie hangs down about 15 cm further than the narrow end.

2. Pull the wide end of the tie over the thin part, then tuck it back underneath, so the seam of the wide end is facing out.

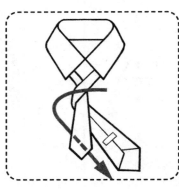

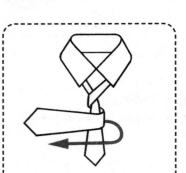

3. Bring the wide end back over the top of the narrow end, as shown here.

4. Push the wide end of the tie through the loop at your neck.

5. Now push the wide end of the tie down through the loop you have just made.

6. Tighten the knot by holding on to the narrow end and sliding the knot up to your neck.

SKILL SUGGESTION

You might have to wear a tie to school or to family events. If you have got a really special occasion to attend, and you want to make sure that you look super-smart and stylish, why not swap your tie for a bow tie? You can find out how to tie one of these in **Skill 13**.

SNEEZE SENSIBLY

Sneezing is your body's brilliant way of expelling germs – at up to 150 kilometres per hour! Sadly, it's not so brilliant for anyone on the receiving end, so here's how you can avoid spreading germs when you sneeze:

1. When you feel a sneeze coming, turn your face away from anyone around you.

2. Grab a fresh, strong tissue and sneeze into it. Make sure the tissue covers your nose and mouth completely, so droplets do not escape from the sides.

3. Fold the tissue over and throw it away – preferably into a bin with a lid. Wash your hands thoroughly (see **Skill 3**) to ensure there are no germs on them.

WARNING

Never share your tissues or hankies with anyone else, even your best friend. You will spread thousands of nasty germs.

SKILL 8

CUT YOUR TOENAILS

Long toenails are not big or clever. They get dirty and carry germs, too. In fact, they're pretty gross! Here's how to keep them short and safe:

1. Soak your feet thoroughly to remove any dirt and soften your nails. This makes the nails easier to trim.

2. Use nail clippers and start with your big toe. Put the nail end between the clippers and squeeze them to cut it.

3. Cut straight across the toenail, without catching the skin around it. This will stop you from getting ingrown nails, which cut into the sides of the nail bed and can be very painful.

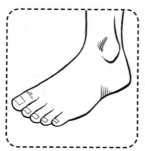

4. Trim all of your toenails in this way, so they are about the same length, as shown here.

5. Wash your feet again in hot, soapy water and dry them thoroughly. To keep your feet fresh, wear clean, cotton socks, and change them every day.

SKILL 9

BEAT STINKY SHOES

Do you have the stinky-shoe blues? If your smelly trainers could knock out your mates, then it's time to sort out the poisonous pong. Here's how:

OPTION 1: BARBECUE IT

★ Put some unused lumps of charcoal from a barbecue bag into a pair of pop socks – ask your mum or sister for an old pair – and tie them at the top.

★ Place one pop sock in each shoe and leave overnight. In the morning, you should be enjoying the sweet smell of success.

OPTION 2: REALLY AP-PEEL-ING

★ The next time you eat a juicy orange, save the peel.

★ Place the orange peel inside your shoes and leave overnight.

★ Put the peel in the compost bin or waste bin the next morning, and be amazed by your fresh, zingy footwear.

OPTION 3: DO THE SODA SPRINKLE

★ Look in your kitchen for some bicarbonate of soda (a white powder used in baking), or ask an adult for some. Put a teaspoonful in each shoe and shake it.

★ Leave overnight then shake out the powdery soda into the bin.

★ It will have soaked up the smell during the night, leaving your shoes smelling great.

OPTION 4: FRRRREEZING

★ Wrap your stinky shoes in a plastic bag and tie a knot in it to secure.

★ Place the bag in your freezer and leave it overnight.

★ The smelly bacteria in your shoes will be destroyed by the icy temperatures, leaving them smelling fresh and clean.

★ Don't forget to let your shoes warm up before you put them on, or your feet will be frozen, too!

SKILL 10

LACE AND TIE A SHOE

There are hundreds and hundreds of different ways to lace up a pair of shoes. You could spend your life working out all of them, or you could follow these super-simple steps:

1. Push one end of the lace down through the bottom eyelet and thread it straight across and up into the other eyelet.

2. Pull up the lace, so that both ends are the same length.

3. Take one end and thread it across the tongue of the shoe and down into the next eyelet.

4. Continue criss-crossing with the lace, going into the eyelet that is diagonally opposite each time.

5. Once you've done one end, repeat with the other, so the lace criss-crosses completely and all the eyelets are threaded.

Now it's time to make sure you know how to tie the laces.

6. Take both ends of the lace and cross them over.

7. Put your finger under where the lace crosses, tuck one end of the lace under to make a knot, then pull it tight.

8. Place your index finger on the knot to keep it secure.

9. Make a loose loop with one of the laces and hold it at the base with two fingers.

10. Pull the other lace around the base of the loop in a circle, then tuck the middle of this lace back through the circle to make another loop.

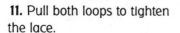

11. Pull both loops to tighten the lace.

★

PACK A SCHOOL BAG

**Lugging around a school bag doesn't have to be
a pain in the neck – or shoulders. Follow these steps
to make sure your load is as light as possible:**

CHOOSE A BAG ...

★ ... with sturdy, padded straps
or a good handle.

★ ... with lots of pockets, strong
zips and waterproof outer layer.

1. Load your bag so the contents won't
move around. Place the heaviest items in the area of the bag
that's closest to your body. Put objects that you use the most
in pockets, so you can find them easily.

2. Make sure the load inside your
bag is distributed evenly. If you've
got a backpack, use both shoulder
straps to carry it – this will stop
your back aching.

3. Avoid carrying too much stuff.
If you can't pick up your bag
easily, it's too heavy. Get used to
emptying your bag out often
– it's amazing how much junk
can build up!

SKILL 12

ZAP A ZIT

Zits – no one likes them but everyone gets them, even superstars. So, if you wake up with one on your face, check out these steps:

1. Wash your hands thoroughly, see **Skill 3**. Look into a mirror that is positioned in a well-lit area.

2. Does the spot have a white or black 'head' on it? If not, rub some spot cream into it and leave it alone. Otherwise, move on to **step 3**.

3. Wrap both your index fingers in clean tissue and apply gentle pressure either side of the zit, to try and squeeze out the white pus inside.

4. Clean the zit and the area around it with soap and water, then rub in some anti-spot cream.

SKILL SUGGESTION

To help keep your skin smooth and spot free, eat foods with lots of vitamin C, such as oranges, strawberries and tomatoes; vitamin E, such as olive oil, sunflower seeds and hazelnuts; and vitamin A, such as cheese, eggs and fish.
See **Skill 19** for help in eating healthily.

TIE A BOW TIE

You may not wear a bow tie every day, but if you want to look as suave and sophisticated as James Bond, tying one is a very useful skill to master.

1. Stand in front of a mirror with the bow tie around your neck. Leave one side longer than the other by about 4 cm.

2. Take the longer side and cross it over the other one, then loop it underneath and through.

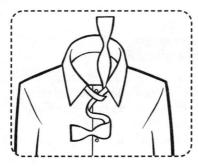

3. Fold the shorter side, as shown here, with the end at the front.

4. Hold the fold in place with one finger and bring the long side down over it, making a loop.

5. Fold this side, as shown here, with the end at the back.

6. Finally, push this fold through the back of the loop that you made in **step 4**, keeping hold of both ends.

7. You should now be able to see your bow tie taking shape. For the final shaken-not-stirred look, adjust both ends and tighten your perfect bow tie.

SKILL 14

HAVE SHINY SHOES

Whether you wear leather shoes to school, or just on special occasions. Here's how you can make them really shine:

1. Spread some sheets of old newspaper on the floor where you will be doing the polishing. Take the laces out of your shoes.

2. Wipe off any mud or dust with a damp cloth, and allow your shoes to dry.

3. Wrap a soft, dry cloth around your index and middle fingers and dip it in some clear shoe polish, or shoe polish that matches the colour of your shoes.

4. Apply the polish to the shoe by rubbing in small circular motions, starting from the heel, until the whole shoe is covered in a thin layer. Now do the other shoe. Leave your shoes for as long as you can to absorb the polish.

5. Use a shoe brush to make the polish shine. Brush your shoes in quick sideways movements. This is called 'buffing'.

6. Repeat **steps 4** and **5** to build up the shine on your shoes.

SKILL 15

MANAGE YOUR MONEY

Ever wondered why some of your friends seem to have pots of cash, while others are always on the scrounge? It all comes down to the skill of money management. Here are some top tips:

★ Get a tin with a lock, or a piggy bank, to keep your money in. Keep it in a safe place and top it up with any pocket money or birthday money you get.

★ To earn some extra cash, ask your parents if they will pay you a small amount for doing chores, such as washing the car (see **Skill 37**) or doing the laundry (**see Skill 60**).

★ If you've got your eye on something you want to buy, avoid the temptation to splurge on sweets and comics the minute you get your pocket money.

★ If you're serious about saving, ask your parents to help you open a young person's bank account. The bank rewards you for saving rather than spending by paying you a small percentage of your savings as a bonus. This is called 'interest'. So sit back and watch your money grow!

SKILL 16

TELL THE TIME ON A 24-HOUR CLOCK

If you're planning an outing or booking a trip, you'll notice that most timetables display times in the 24-hour clock – e.g. 15:35 or 19:17. To make sure you're always on time, here's all you need to know about reading a 24-hour clock:

★ The numbers before the **:** refer to the hour, and the numbers after the **:** tell you how many minutes past the hour it is.

★ Times between midnight and noon are shown as 00:00 to 12:00. Midnight is 00:00 – think of it as the start of a new day.

★ Times after noon and before midnight are shown as 12:01 to 23:59.

★ Whenever you see any numbers before the **:** that are larger than 12, subtract 12 from this number to work out what time it is. For example, 15:30 is half-past three in the afternoon, because 15 – 12 = 3, while 03:30 is half-past three in the morning.

SKILL 17

BANISH HICCUPS

Doctors know what hiccups are (they're muscle spasms in your throat and chest), but so far no one has come up with a foolproof way of getting rid of them. Here are five possible ways to beat hiccups. Try them out and see which one works for you:

★ Take a deep breath and hold it for as long as you can. Repeat until cured.

★ Swallow as quickly and as often as you can, or glug down little sips of water quickly.

★ Eat a large spoonful of peanut butter. (Don't try this method if you're allergic to peanuts.)

★ Suck on something sour, such as a lemon or lime slice.

★ Plug your ears then swallow some water slowly.

SKILL 18

AVOID TRAVEL SICKNESS

Nothing ruins a journey like being sick. If you get queasy just thinking about stepping into a plane, boat or car, this advice is especially for you:

SEATING SOLUTION

In a car: Sit in the front passenger seat if you can.
On a boat: Sit up on deck, so you're in the fresh air.
On a plane: Get a window seat over a wing,
if possible, as this is where it's least bumpy.

DO: Drink plenty of water throughout the journey to help you stay hydrated.

DON'T: Read or play computer games.

DO: Get plenty of fresh air if you can. Open a window or walk up on deck.

DON'T: Eat greasy or sweet snacks before you travel.

SKILL 19

EAT A HEALTHY DIET

You may wish you could eat chips for every meal, but having a balanced diet is really important to help you grow and stay healthy and full of energy. Use the chart below to help you eat right every day:

You should eat:
Five portions of fruit
and vegetables
a day.

You can eat lots of:
Pasta, bread, rice,
noodles, potatoes
and cereals.

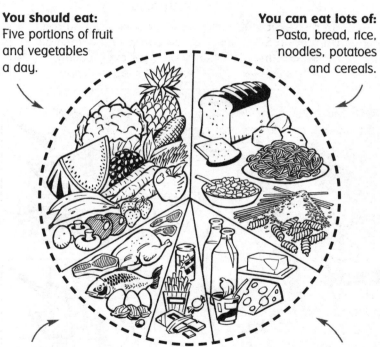

Make sure you include some:
Red meat,
chicken, eggs,
nuts and fish.

Try to cut down on:
Fizzy drinks, chips, cakes,
biscuits, crisps, sweets
and chocolate.

You can eat small amounts of:
Cheese, milk
and yogurt.

MASTER-CHEF

SKILL 20

BE SAFE IN THE KITCHEN

Before you start whipping up any delicious masterpieces in the kitchen, you've got to know how to beat bacteria and deal with dangerous equipment to keep your cooking clean and safe.

BE HOT ON HYGIENE

★ Before you touch any ingredients, wash your hands well (see **Skill 3**).

★ If you're going to be cooking or preparing food, put plasters on any cuts or scrapes on your hands to stop infection.

★ Make sure that when you unpack the shopping, you store meat, fish and dairy produce in the fridge so it doesn't spoil.

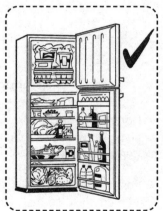

★ After you have touched raw food, especially meat, wash your hands thoroughly.

DON'T FEEL THE BURN

★ Always use oven gloves when handling hot plates, pans or oven doors.

★ Never leave the handles of hot saucepans overhanging the front of the cooker or a hot part of the hob, as they might get knocked off or burn you.

★ Never lean over electric or gas rings that are switched on.

★ Lean back slightly as you pour hot liquids so you don't get scalded by the steam.

SHARPEN UP YOUR ACT

★ Don't leave sharp knives in washing-up water, as they could be hidden by bubbles.

★ Pass scissors and knives to people handle-end first, so they don't cut themselves on the blade.

★ Carry knives with the blade pointing downwards so that you are safe if you trip over.

★ Use chopping boards placed on flat, stable surfaces to prepare ingredients.

SKILL 21

SET A TABLE

If you are asked to set the table, make sure you do it properly, so you and your family can enjoy the meal in style.

A: Forks sit to the left of the plate. Place the fork for the starter on the outside, then the larger fork for the main course on its right.

B: Knives go to the right of the plate, with the starter knife on the outside, and the larger knife for the main course to the left of it.

C: A dessert spoon should be placed along the top of the plate, with the handle pointing towards the knives. If your dessert needs a fork to eat it with, place this just below the spoon, with the prongs pointing right.

D: Put glasses above the dessert spoon and to the right. You will need one glass for a soft drink and another for water.

E: Finally, place a folded napkin to the left of the forks and prepare to wow your dinner guests.

SKILL 22

BOIL AN EGG

What's not to like about boiled eggs? They're super-tasty, super-filling and you can rustle them up in about five minutes. On your marks, get set, go:

WARNING

Always ask an adult before using the hob or boiling water.

1. Pour enough cold water into a saucepan to cover your egg and turn on the heat underneath it.

2. Wait for the water to boil. Gently lower your egg into the pan on a tablespoon.

SKILL SUGGESTION

Stop the egg from cracking by pricking the bigger end with a pin before you put it in the pan. This will allow the steam to escape.

3. Turn the heat down so the water is bubbling gently.

4. Set your timer for four minutes if you want your egg with a runny yolk, or six minutes if you want it to be squidgy and firm.

5. Use the spoon to fish your egg out when the cooking time is up. (Don't forget to turn off the hob.)

6. Place it in an egg cup, with the fattest end at the bottom. Cut the top off the shell with the edge of a teaspoon and serve with buttered toast cut into fingers.

SKILL 23

PEEL A POTATO

Bored of baked potatoes? For chips, mashed, roast or fried spuds, you're going to have to master the art of potato peeling. Here's how:

WARNING

Take special care when using a sharp peeler.

1. If you're right-handed, hold the potato in your left hand (or the other way round if you're left-handed) and the peeler in your other hand.

2. Hold the peeler firmly. Position it so that the blade is at the top of the potato.

3. Apply pressure with the blade of the peeler and scrape it slowly and carefully away from you, removing a strip of skin from the potato.

4. Repeat **steps 2** and **3** until you've peeled all the skin off the potato.

5. Put the peelings in your compost bin or waste bin.

SKILL 24

COOK GREAT SPAGHETTI

**To make pasta fantastica,
follow these simple steps:**

WARNING

Always ask an adult before using the hob or boiling water.

1. Fill a large pan with cold water. Turn on the heat and wait until the water is boiling.

2. Add a large pinch of salt to the water for flavour, and add a splash of olive oil – this will stop the pasta sticking to the pan.

3. Carefully add the pasta to the pan. You should allow 75 g of pasta for each adult and 50 g for each child. It will soften as it hits the hot water, so carefully push it down with a wooden spoon until it is all under the water in the pan.

4. Set your timer for nine minutes.

5. While the pasta is cooking, stir it several times to make sure it is not sticking to the bottom of the pan.

6. After the timer has gone off, fish out a strand of spaghetti using a fork. Blow on it to make sure you don't burn your mouth, then taste it. It should be soft on the outside and firm on the inside. If the pasta is too hard, leave it to cook for a bit longer.

7. Once the pasta is properly cooked, place a colander in your sink and turn the hob off. Carefully pour the pasta into the colander to drain, then serve the pasta piping hot.

Did You Know? Some people flick a few strands of their spaghetti against a wall to see if it's ready. If it sticks, it's done. Please check with an adult before you cover the walls with pasta!

SKILL SUGGESTION

Try pepping up your finished pasta with ...

★ ... butter and black pepper.
★ ... basil leaves and tomatoes.

SKILL 25

MAKE TERRIFIC TEA

A perfect cup of tea is sure to put a smile on anyone's face. Here's how to make one:

WARNING

Always take extra care when using boiling water.

1. Fill the kettle with cold water then turn on the power.

2. Line up the mugs or teacups, teapot, spoons and sugar. Leave the milk in the fridge until later.

3. Pour some warm water from the tap into the teapot. Carefully swirl the water around for 30 seconds then pour it away.

A warm pot will help the tea to release its colour and flavour.

4. Put spoonfuls of loose tea, or teabags into the pot – one spoonful, or teabag, for each person and one extra.

5. After the kettle has boiled, pour the water into the pot. Pour slowly away from yourself and be careful not to scald yourself in the steam.

6. Stir the tea in the pot, then leave it to brew for three minutes – any longer than that and the tea will start to taste bitter.

7. Pour a splash of chilled milk into the mugs or teacups then pour in the tea. If you have used loose tea you will need to hold a strainer over the top of each mug or cup as you pour, to catch the tea leaves.

8. Add sugar to sweeten the tea if your guests ask for some, stir it in thoroughly and serve.

SKILL 26

PEEL AN ORANGE

Peeling an orange doesn't have to be a long, messy struggle. For a simple way to tuck in, you'll need a sharp knife and an orange. Here's what to do:

WARNING

Take extra care when using a sharp knife.

1. Place the orange on its side on a chopping board. Roll it around to loosen the skin.

2. Slice the top and bottom off the orange.

3. Carefully cut the orange into equal-sized quarters.

4. Peel each quarter of the orange and tuck into the juicy fruit. Make sure you eat it over a plate to catch the extra juice.

SKILL SUGGESTION

Keep the peel from your orange, and turn to **Skill 9** for a stink-busting way to use it.

SKILL 27

CRACK AN EGG CHEF-STYLE

Impress your friends and family with your kitchen skills by mastering the one-handed egg break:

1. Get a bowl or cup ready then pick up your egg.

2. Hold it in your strongest hand with your thumb on one side, your first finger hooked over the top of the egg, and your middle and third fingers on the other side.

3. Tap the egg firmly against the rim of the bowl or cup. Try not to tap too hard. The aim is to crack the egg – not shatter it.

4. Place your middle finger over the crack and pull the front of the shell upwards. At the same time, use your thumb to push gently against the egg shell to move the two halves in opposite directions.

5. As the egg pours out into the bowl or cup below, raise your hand briskly.

SKILL 28

CHOP AN ONION

This is a quick and safe way to chop an onion – minimum fuss, minimum mess, guaranteed.

WARNING

Use extra care when handling sharp knives.

---

1. Put the onion on its side on a chopping board, with the root facing left and the top facing right. Reverse this if you are left-handed.

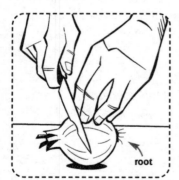

2. Cut off the top, but leave the root intact. This will help keep the onion together as you chop it and will reduce the stinging vapours that can make you cry.

3. Peel the papery layer of brown skin off the onion.

4. Place the onion's cut side flat on the chopping board, and slice it in half through the root.

5. Take one half and, with the knife pointing towards the root, make slices all the way along the length of the onion. Make sure the tip of your knife reaches the root, but doesn't cut through it.

6. Use your fingers to hold the sliced bits together, then slice the onion widthways until it's all nicely diced.

7. Repeat **steps 5** and **6** on the other half of the onion.

SKILL SUGGESTION

Chopping onions can make even the bravest boys well up. Here are some anti-tear tips:

★ Don't rub your eyes while chopping. Wait until you've washed your hands.

★ Stick your tongue out while chopping the onion.

★ Soak the onion in water for 30 minutes before you start chopping.

SKILL 29

GET PANCAKE POWER

Pancakes are simple to make and delicious to eat – not just on Pancake Day, but on any day! Follow these steps to make and flip a perfect pancake:

WARNING

Ask an adult before using the hob.

1. Sift the flour and salt into a large mixing bowl.

2. Make a small hollow in the flour and break the eggs into it.

3. Mix the eggs and flour together with a whisk or a fork.

4. In a jug, mix the water and the milk together.

YOU WILL NEED

- 110 g plain flour
- 200 ml milk
- 75 ml water
- 50 g unsalted butter
- 2 eggs
- a pinch of salt
(Makes 12 to 14)

5. Gradually pour the milk and water mixture into the bowl, whisking all the time. You should now have a smooth batter with no lumps of flour.

6. Melt the butter in a frying pan, pour it into the batter and whisk. This frying pan will be used to cook and flip your pancakes, so make sure it's not too heavy.

7. Turn the heat up under the pan, and spoon a ladleful of the batter into the centre.

8. Tilt the pan around so that the batter covers the whole surface in a thin layer.

Now it's time to do some fantastic flipping.

9. Turn the heat down and let the pancake cook on one side for about a minute.

10. Shake the pan from side to side to check that the pancake is not sticking. You may need to gently slide a spatula underneath to get it sliding around properly.

11. Grip the handle of the pan in both hands and lift it off the hob. Flick the pan upwards in a smooth, scooping motion so that the pancake flips up and all the way over.

12. Let the pancake cook for one minute on the other side, then serve with lemon juice and sugar.

SKILL 30

MAKE A SMOOTHIE

Smoothies are delicious, fun to make and super-healthy too. Read on to find out how to become a smoothie operator:

WARNING

Ask an adult before using a blender.

---

1. Peel the banana, then wash and slice the strawberries and banana into chunks. The smaller the chunks, the smoother your smoothie will be.

2. Put the ice in a clean food bag then bash it into bits with a rolling pin.

YOU WILL NEED

- 1 banana
- 200 g strawberries
- 120 ml milk
- 250 ml vanilla yogurt
- 4 large ice cubes
(Serves 2)

3. Put the fruit in the blender first, followed by the crushed ice. Put the lid on the blender, then quickly blend the two together. Switch off the blender, take the lid off and pour the milk and yogurt over the top.

4. Put the lid back on, and begin blending slowly then turn up the speed. If your smoothie looks more like a 'lumpie', switch off the blender, stir the mixture with a spoon then blend again.

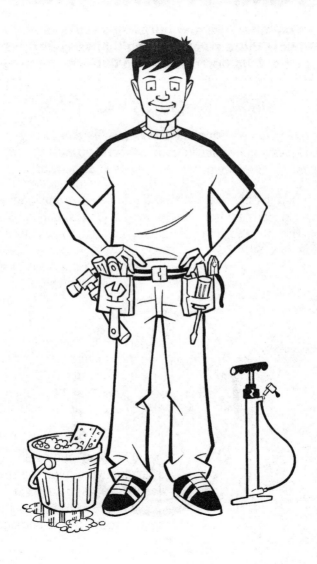

DO IT YOURSELF

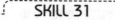

PUMP UP BIKE TYRES

Getting a flat tyre on your bike is really annoying. Follow these steps and you'll have your tyres pumped up and ready to go again in no time:

'WHEELY' IMPORTANT KNOWLEDGE

If you ride your bike often, the air pressure in your tyres will gradually reduce. Eventually you might end up with a sad-looking flat tyre, which is dangerous to cycle with.

To help you get back on the road quickly, look at the diagram below, and learn the names of all the different parts of a bike wheel. This will also come in handy when you need to fix a puncture (see **Skill 35**).

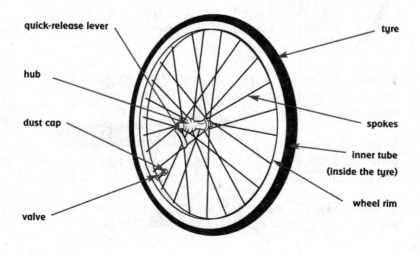

quick-release lever

tyre

hub

dust cap

spokes

inner tube
(inside the tyre)

wheel rim

valve

GET PUMPING

1. Lean your bike against a wall, or balance it on its stand.

2. Find the valve and remove the 'dust cap,' (use the diagram on the opposite page to help you locate it). Once you've unscrewed it, put it somewhere safe, like your back pocket.

3. Push your bike pump on to the valve stem and secure it.

There are different types of bike pump – some models screw on to the valve, while others use a clamp lever. Read the manual for your pump to find out how yours works.

4. Start pumping with a push-and-pull action, and keep going until your bike tyre is firm to the touch. Be careful not to over inflate the tyre.

5. Take the pump off the valve and screw the dust cap back on.

6. Repeat **steps 2** to **5** on the other tyre.

SKILL SUGGESTION

Make sure you check your tyres regularly. If you find that they keep on going flat, you may have something called a 'slow puncture'. To find out how to fix a puncture, see **Skill 35**.

TIGHTEN A SCREW

**Knowing exactly how to use a screwdriver
is a really useful skill. Here's how to tighten a screw:**

BEFORE YOU START

Check that your screwdriver is the right type and size
for the screw you need to tighten. Here are the most common
screw head shapes, and the screwdrivers that match them.

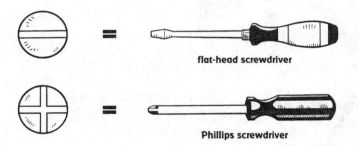

flat-head screwdriver

Phillips screwdriver

1. Grip the handle of the screwdriver in your writing hand.

2. Place the end of the screwdriver into the notch on the
screw head.

3. Turn the screwdriver clockwise to tighten the screw. The rhyme
'Righty Tighty' will help you remember which way to turn.

4. Continue turning the screwdriver until the screw is held
securely in place.

SKILL 33

THREAD A NEEDLE

**Before you can make repairs to any of your clothes,
you need to know how to thread a needle.
Here's how to do it:**

1. Cut a piece of thread about the same length as your arm from the reel.

SKILL SUGGESTION

Licking the end of the thread before you push it through the eye of the needle will help.

2. Hold up the needle and tilt it, so you can see the hole in it, called the 'eye'. Take the freshly cut end of the thread and carefully push it through the eye – this might take a few goes.

3. Once the thread appears on the other side of the eye, take hold of it with the tips of your fingers and pull it until you have got a 'tail' of 5 to 10 cm.

4. Tie two knots on top of each other at the long end of the thread. This will stop it from being pulled all the way through the fabric while you're sewing. Now you are ready for any emergency sewing projects.

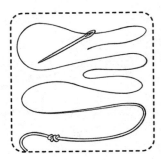

SKILL 34

MEND A RIPPED SEAM

Ripped jeans might look cool, but a ripped shirt or jumper is plain cold. Luckily, if it has torn along a seam, it's pretty easy to fix. Here's how:

1. Turn your shirt inside out and find the rip in the seam.

2. Carefully pin the two edges of the seam against each other.

3. Turn the shirt the right way out to make sure the join looks okay, and adjust if necessary.

4. Use thread that matches the stitching in your shirt, then thread your needle (see **Skill 33**).

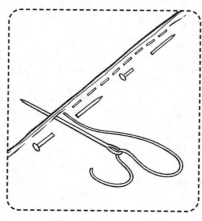

5. Working on the inside of the shirt, start stitching a little way before the start of the rip. Push the needle down through the existing seam and weave it back up again a little way along, then pull the thread through. Secure the end of your thread by making a few small stitches in one place.

6. Continue this down-and-up motion along the length of the rip. This is called a 'running stitch'. Be careful not to pull the thread too tight, or the fabric will wrinkle.

7. To make sure your stitches are really secure, you need to do something called 'overstitching'. Here's how to do it.

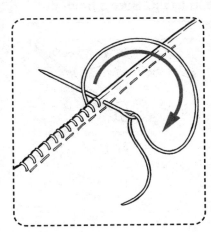

From the point where you finished your running stitch, insert the needle through one side of the seam, and push it straight out the other side.

Loop the thread over the seam and reinsert the needle on the same side as before, a little further down. Continue in this way back along the length of your running stitches.

8. To finish, sew three or four small stitches over the top of one another.

9. Pull the thread tight and snip it off, then turn the shirt the right way out and admire your sewing skill.

SKILL 35

FIX A PUNCTURE

Getting a puncture is a real pain – no amount of pumping will keep your tyre firm. So follow these steps to find out how to fix a puncture properly:

SKILL SUGGESTION

Use the diagram of a bike wheel in **Skill 31** when tackling a puncture. It will help you to identify all the parts of your wheel and get that puncture patched up more quickly.

YOU WILL NEED

• the manual for your bike
• a puncture repair kit including: rubber patches, glue, sandpaper, tyre levers (optional)
• a bowl of water
• a bike pump
• a piece of chalk
• a cloth

---

1. First you need to check that you definitely have a puncture, and that your flat tyre has not been caused by a leaky valve.

To test the valve to see if it leaks, unscrew the dust cap on the valve of the flat tyre, and hold a cup of water up to the valve, so that it is in the water.

If you see bubbles in the water, the valve is leaking and it's not a puncture causing your tyre to go flat. In this case, you need to take your bike to a bicycle repair shop. If there are no bubbles in the water, go to **step 2**.

2. Look closely at the flat tyre. Can you spot any sharp items sticking out? If you can see something pointy lurking, like a screw or a nail, carefully pull it out of the tyre, wrap it in a tissue and throw it away. Then move on to **step 3**.

3. Unfasten the brakes. This is called 'disengaging', and you will need to refer to the detailed instructions in your bike's manual to find out how to do this.

4. Unscrew or press on the tyre valve to let any last bits of air out of the 'inner tube' – the tube that sits inside the tyre. Check your bike's manual to find out if you need to press it or unscrew it.

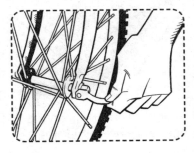

5. Take the wheel off by pulling the quick-release lever on the wheel outwards. If your bike does not have a lever like this, look in the manual to find out how to remove the wheel.

6. Carefully ease the inner tube out from inside the wheel rim. If you've got tyre levers, use these to help you to prise the tube out. Push the valve up and out through the hole in the rim too, so you don't risk tearing the inner tube. You may need to unscrew it first.

tyre levers   wheel rim

7. Now you need to locate the puncture. To do this, hold the inner tube up to your ear and listen for a hiss of escaping air, or hold it next to your cheek and see if you can feel a puff of air rushing out through the hole.

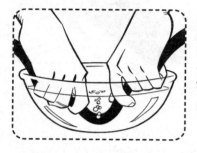

If you can't find the hole like this, dip sections of the inner tube into the bowl of water and watch for bubbles appearing. This will tell you where the puncture is.

8. Mark the place where the hole is with your chalk, so you'll be able to find it again. Then use the cloth to dry the inner tube.

9. Rub the area around the hole with the sandpaper from your puncture repair kit, to roughen it up.

10. Spread a blob of glue over the hole and leave it until it is almost dry, but still 'tacky' to the touch.

11. Take a patch from your puncture repair kit and put a small blob of glue on its 'contact surface'. Wait until this, too, is tacky to the touch.

12. Place the patch over the hole and hold it firmly for a few minutes to secure it.

13. Smooth it down to remove any bubbles and peel away the backing sheet on the patch.

14. Use chalk to dust the inner tube, putting plenty around the patch, as this will stop it from sticking to the inside of the tyre.

15. Use your tyre levers to prise the tyre away from the rim and look inside for any glass or nails. Carefully remove any that you find, wrap them in a tissue and throw them away.

16. Pump up the inner tube very slightly. This will make it easier to fit back on to the wheel rim.

17. Push part of the inner tube under the tyre. Make sure that the valve is aligned with the hole in the rim, and gently slot it back through. It should be pointing straight down towards the wheel hub.

18. Tuck the rest of the inner tube under the tyre, and pump up the tyre until it's firm (see **Skill 31**).

19. Put the wheel back on the bike by positioning it between the brake pads and closing the quick-release lever. If you don't have a lever, refer to your bike's manual for how to do this correctly.

20. Re-engage your bike's brakes – check the manual to find out how to do this – and test that your brakes are working.

SKILL 36

SEW ON A BUTTON

Follow these steps to make sure that missing buttons are a thing of the past:

1. Match the new button and thread with the remaining ones. Thread a needle with about 40 cms of your chosen thread (see **Skill 33**).

2. Place the button in position on the outside of the garment then push the needle up from the inside, through one of the holes in the button.

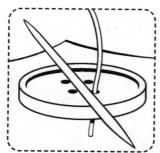

3. Place a cocktail stick across the top of your button. This will keep your stitches loose and allow the button to move around enough to go through a buttonhole.

4. Take the thread across the cocktail stick and down into the next hole in the button to create a small loop. Then bring the needle back up through the first hole and repeat this stitch three or four times.

5. Repeat **steps 2** and **4**, finishing with your thread between the button and the fabric.

6. Pull out the cocktail stick, then pull the button gently to make a space underneath it. Wind the thread around the thread underneath the button about 20 times to lift it slightly off the surface of the fabric, as shown.

7. To secure your button, push the needle back down to the inside of the garment, then make several small stitches on top of each other.

8. Snip off any loose ends and you're done.

SHANK BUTTONS

★ Your button might have a small loop of metal or plastic on its back rather than four holes – this is called a shank.

★ If you're sewing on a button like this, you don't need to worry about **step 3**, or **steps 5** and **6**.

★ To start, push your needle through from the back of the garment, then thread it through the loop on the back of the button.

★ Make a small stitch in the fabric to secure the button in place. Then push the needle through the loop in the button, and make another stitch on top of the first one.

★ Repeat this four or five times, then finish with **steps 7** and **8**.

SKILL 37

WASH A CAR

When you're looking for a little extra cash, why not offer to wash the car? Here's how to do it:

1. Loosen the top layer of grime by hosing the car down or pouring buckets of cold water over it.

2. Fill one of the buckets with a mixture of warm water and car shampoo, and the other with clean, cold water.

YOU WILL NEED
- rubber gloves
- 2 buckets
- a hose (optional)
- car shampoo
- a sponge
- a stiff brush
- a chamois leather (or a clean, soft cloth)
- car wax
- 2 clean, dry cloths

3. Wearing rubber gloves, dip the sponge into the warm, soapy water. Start cleaning the roof then work your way down the body of the car.

4. Don't forget to clean the bumpers, wheel arches and underneath the windscreen wipers.

5. The wheels are usually the dirtiest part of the car, so wash them last. Use the brush to get rid of any stubborn dirt.

6. Every time the sponge gets dirty, dip it in the bucket of cold water to rinse it. Change the water in the bucket when it gets too grimy.

7. Rinse off all the shampoo with the hose, or a bucket of clean, cold water.

8. Dry the car's paintwork with the chamois leather.

9. Dab one of the clean, dry cloths into the car wax and work it slowly into the paintwork in little circular motions. The wax will make the paintwork look cloudy. Use the other clean, soft cloth to rub the wax until the car shines.

SKILL SUGGESTION

For an extra-special clean (and to earn a bonus from your folks), finish the job by vacuuming the seats and the floor inside the car.

SKILL 38

CATCH A SPIDER

Be heroic in your household by fearlessly trapping and releasing spiders. It's easy!

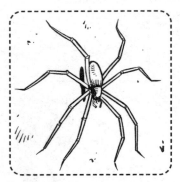

1. Wait until the spider is on a wall, window or other flat surface.

2. Hold a piece of paper in one hand and place a glass over the spider – make sure you don't squash its legs.

3. Wait for the spider to scuttle towards the bottom of the glass. Once it's there, slip the paper under the rim of the glass, making sure the opening is completely covered.

4. Turn the glass so that the paper is on top and carry it outside. When you're away from the house, put the glass upside down on the ground.

5. Tap the glass so the spider drops on to the paper then lift up the glass and let the mini-beast wander away.

SKILL 39

LIFT HEAVY THINGS

Don't be a superhero when lifting heavy objects – you might end up hurting your back. Instead, follow these smart steps:

1. Take a good look at the object you're lifting. Check for handles to help you grip it. If you think it might be extremely heavy, or it is an odd or bulky shape, ask a friend to help you.

2. If you're going to be moving the object, trace your route in advance and remove anything that might be in your way.

3. Once you've got a clear path, stand squarely in front of the object. Your feet should be a shoulder-width apart, with one leg slightly forwards, so that your body is well balanced.

4. Bend your knees and, keeping your back as straight as you can, lower yourself down until you can get a good grip on the object.

Practise bending and straightening up again with your back straight before you pick up the object.

5. Let your leg muscles do the work when picking the object up. Stand up in one, smooth movement, and keep your back straight.

6. Raise your arms slightly and keep the object close to your body, to avoid putting strain on your back. Keep your head up.

7. Use small steps to reach your destination. Take it slowly and put the object down for a breather if you can't carry it the full distance all in one go.

8. When you're ready to put the heavy object down, plant your feet apart, then use your legs and knees again to lower the object. Keep your back as straight as you can. Never reach across or twist to put the item down.

SKILL 40

TEST A SMOKE ALARM

**A smoke alarm is one of the most important things in your house. It could save your life if there is a fire by warning you that something's burning.
It's vital that you test it regularly to make sure it's working. Here's how:**

1. Before you test the alarm, warn anyone in the house about what you're going to do.

2. To reach the smoke alarm, use a chair or stepladder. Place it on a smooth, flat surface and ask a friend to hold it steady.

3. Look for the test button on your alarm. It is usually red. Press the button.

4. If the alarm is working, you should hear a loud beep or ring, and it might beep on and off for a while as it resets.

5. Note the date of your test and set a reminder for a week's time. If it is not working, tell an adult in the house and ask them to replace it urgently.

WARNING

Never borrow the battery from a smoke alarm for use in anything else.

SMART SKILLS

SKILL 41

TAKE A GREAT PHOTO

Whether you're a happy snapper or serious about your shots, it's easy to improve the quality of your photographs. You don't need super-expensive kit either, just a few simple tips:

1. If you're taking photos of people, avoid busy or distracting backgrounds – and always look out for plants or buildings that look like they're sticking out of people's heads. These are best avoided.

2. When taking pictures of buildings or scenery, most people take landscape (long and wide) pictures. Vary your snaps by trying dramatic portrait (tall and thin) compositions.

3. Try to get on the same level as the subject of your photo rather than an awkward angle looking up or down.

4. Use the flash, even during sunny days outside. If you do this, it fills in dark, shadowed areas with light.

SKILL 42

PITCH A TENT

Before you set out on your camping adventures, you need to know how to pitch a tent. Be extra prepared and practise in the garden before you go. Remember, every tent is different, so keep your tent's assembly instructions with you:

1. Choose your spot. Look for somewhere flat, clear of roots and rocks and with no signs of animal tracks or nests. Try not to pitch on very low ground or near water, in case of flooding.

2. Lay out the tent parts and instructions near your chosen location and check that nothing is missing.

3. If your tent has a groundsheet, stretch this out flat on the ground.

4. Lie the tent flat over the top of the groundsheet and make sure that the entrance is zipped shut.

5. Assemble all the metal supporting poles your tent needs and place them in position.

For many tents, this will mean placing the two poles diagonally from corner to corner, and pushing them carefully through the seams in the fabric of the tent.

6. Push the ends of the poles through the loops at the corners of your tent (called 'grommets') and carefully bend them into arches.

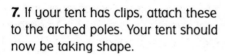

7. If your tent has clips, attach these to the arched poles. Your tent should now be taking shape.

8. Put pegs into the grommets at each of the four corners of your tent and push them into the ground at a 45° angle. You may need to use a mallet to hammer them in if the ground is hard.

9. To waterproof and further secure your tent, place the rain cover (also called the 'fly sheet') over the top of your tent. Make sure that the door of the fly sheet is aligned with the door of the inner tent so you can get in and out.

10. Hook the corners of the fly sheet over the tent pegs in the ground. Check for any other grommets on the fly sheet and peg them into the ground, too, so the fabric is taut.

11. Finally, for extra security, pull the ropes on the fly sheet until they are taut, and peg them into the ground.

PREPARE FOR A TEST

Tests don't have to be too trying. The secret is to make sure you're prepared well in advance:

★ Read through your work slowly and test yourself after every page.

★ Get a good night's sleep before your test – it will help you to stay calm.

★ Don't cram in lots of revision at the last minute – you won't be able to take it all in.

★ Pack your bag with your pencil case and papers the night before, so you're not rushing around in the morning.

★ Don't skip breakfast before your test – you need to feed your brain as well as your body.

SKILL 44

TIE A CLOVE HITCH

A clove hitch is a useful knot to master for tying ropes around poles and railings. Here's how to get the knack:

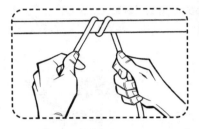

1. Wrap the rope twice over the railing, as shown.

2. Bring the left-hand end of the rope across to the right at the front of the railing.

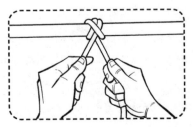

3. Take the end of the rope in your left hand behind the railing and up.

4. Then tuck the end of the rope underneath the loop at the front and pull it tight, so it hangs down at the front of the railing, as shown here.

HAVE GOOD TABLE MANNERS

It's hard to beat eating in front of the telly, but a sit-down meal can be a treat, too. The next time you're about to tuck in, don't forget these DOs and DON'Ts:

DO sit up straight.

DON'T use your fingers.

DON'T spear food off your neighbour's plate without asking.

DON'T talk with your mouth full.

DO put your knife and fork together on your plate once you've finished.

SKILL 46

ANSWER THE PHONE

Follow these steps to make sure you're always terrific on the telephone:

1. When the phone rings, pick it up and say, 'Hello'.

2. Politely ask who is calling if you don't recognize their voice.

3. If they are ringing to talk to someone else in your home, ask them to wait, place the receiver on a flat surface and go and let the person know.

4. If the person is not available, offer to take a message.

5. Repeat the message back to the caller to be sure you've understood everything. Make sure you have the caller's name and number, so that their call can be returned.

6. Thank the caller, then wait for them to ring off and put the phone down. Don't forget to pass the message on to whoever it was meant for.

SKILL SUGGESTION

Keep a pen and a notepad by the phone so that you are always able to write down phone messages.

SKILL 47

ADDRESS AN AUDIENCE

It's only natural to be nervous before standing up in front of a group of people. Luckily, there are lots of ways to take the stress out of addressing an audience. Read on to find out how:

1. Prepare your speech in advance. Even if you only have a few minutes warning, go somewhere quiet to think.

2. If you find memorizing your speech tricky, make short notes on paper as a reminder of the key parts. Try not to rely on these notes too much – looking down at the paper all the time will make you look nervous.

3. Rehearse your speech on your own before you say it in front of an audience. Pay special attention to any long or tricky words you might have to say – the more you practise, the less likely you are to get in a tongue-twisting mess!

4. When you give your speech, try not to walk around or fidget. Keep your hands away from your mouth and talk s-l-o-w-l-y and clearly. If you make a mistake, stop and give yourself time to recover.

5. Smile and look towards your audience. Don't be afraid to make eye contact with individuals in the crowd.

SKILL 48

WRITE A THANK YOU LETTER

Don't forget to say thank you for any presents you receive. Here are some top letter-writing tips:

1. Write your address in the top right-hand corner of the letter, then write the date below it.

2. On the left-hand side, write a greeting to the person reading the letter. If you're writing to an adult, use 'Dear' and then their name.

3. Explain why you are writing. Mention the gift you are thanking them for, say thank you and why you like it.

4. Add some detail about how you are using the gift, or what you are planning to do with it.

5. Bring in some general information about what you have been doing since you last saw the person you are writing to, to make sure your letter is an interesting read.

6. Repeat your thanks and use an informal way of signing off, such as 'lots of love' or 'looking forward to seeing you soon'. Then sign your name. Look at **Skill 50** to find out how to send your letter.

TIE A REEF KNOT

The reef knot is often used for tying bandages, because it is so neat and flat. The Ancient Greeks called it the 'Hercules Knot', because it is so strong and useful. Here's how to tie one:

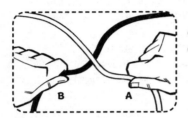

1. Take the two ends of a rope and cross end **A** over the top of end **B**, as shown.

2. Tuck end **A** up behind end **B**. Then bring end **B** over the top of end **A**. Both ends should now be pointing upwards, as shown here.

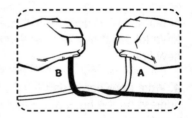

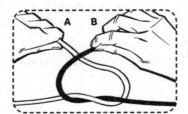

3. Bend end **A** back on itself, and bring end **B** over the top of it.

4. Tuck end **B** behind end **A**, and pull it through the loop that has formed.

5. Pull both ends to tighten the knot.

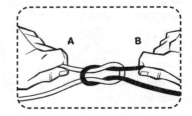

SKILL 50

SEND A PACKAGE

Follow these steps to make sure you never get into a postal pickle:

1. Find an envelope large enough for the item you're sending. If the item is fragile, make sure it is safely protected with layers of bubble wrap or newspaper.

2. Place the empty envelope on a hard, flat surface.

3. In the middle of the front of the envelope, about a third of the way down, write the name of the person who will open the envelope. On the next line, write down the number of their house or flat, followed by the street name. On a new line, jot down the town followed by the county and then the postcode, each on a new line.

4. Write your name and address on the back of the envelope, so it can be returned to you if it doesn't reach its destination. Put the letter or item inside.

5. Take your package to the post office to be weighed so that you can buy the correct postage stamp.

6. Put it in a postbox and wait for a reply.

TIE A BOWLINE

The bowline is used a lot on boats, and is sometimes called 'King of the Knots' because it is so useful. It can even be used to rescue people who have fallen into holes or difficult places to reach. Follow these steps to bowl people over with your bowlines:

1. Cross one end of the rope over the rest of the rope to make a small loop.

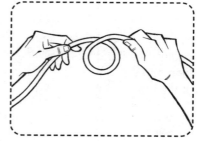

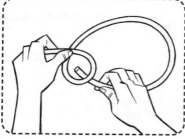

2. Bring the end of the rope back through the loop from behind and pull it through to create another, larger loop.

3. Cross the end that you've just pulled through behind the rest of the rope.

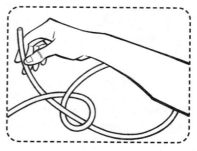

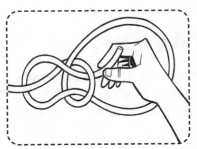

4. Bring this end back to the front of the rope and push it through the first loop that you made.

5. Pinch the end of the rope against the bottom of the larger loop and pull on the long end of the rope to tighten the knot.

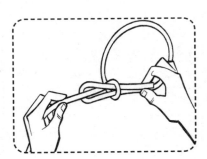

SKILL SUGGESTION

If you find remembering how to tie a bowline is just too tricky, it might help you if you imagine the end of your rope is a mole. In order to tie a bowline, the mole needs to ...

★ ... pop up out of his hole (**step 2**)

★ ... run all the way around a tree (**steps 3** and **4**)

★ ... pop back down into his hole (**steps 4** and **5**)

SKILL 52

WRAP A GIFT

When giving a gift, sometimes the presentation can make it perfect. Follow these steps to find out how to wrap a gift beautifully:

1. If your gift is a difficult shape to wrap, place it in a box before you start.

2. Unroll some giftwrap, and place the box containing the gift upside down in the centre.

3. Bring up the edge of the giftwrap to the middle of the box and then unroll the paper from the other side, bringing it over until it overlaps by about 5 cm. Make a mark on the paper where you need to cut.

4. Cut along the paper in a straight line at the point you marked.

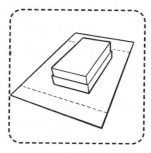

5. Check that there is enough paper at each of the shorter sides to cover the box, but that there is not too much at each end, otherwise folding it into flaps will be tricky. Trim off any excess paper.

6. Bring the long edge of paper that you cut over to the centre of the top of the box and hold it in place with your finger. Then bring the other long edge to the centre so that the two edges overlap. Secure this overlap with sticky tape. Turn the package upside down.

7. Turn the box so that one of the open ends is facing you. Fold the sides in as far as you can without ripping the paper, and crease along the edges of the box so that flaps form at the top and bottom.

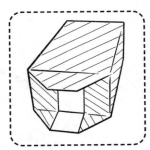

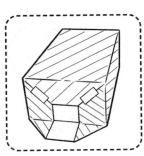

8. Fold the upper flap down and crease it sharply against the side of the box. Put strips of sticky tape on each side of the flap to secure it.

9. Fold the lower flap up and make a sharp crease, then tape it securely to the box. Your wrapping should now look like this.

10. Repeat **steps 7** to **9** with the other end of the box. Add a gift tag so that the person you're giving it to will know who it's from.

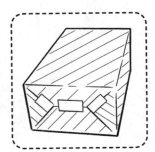

HOME HELP

SKILL 53

PACK SHOPPING BAGS

Packing the shopping at the supermarket is bound to earn you some points with your parents. Here are some helpful hints:

1. Take your own bags with you to the supermarket. Not only is this environmentally friendly, it could also save you money.

2. As you take things out of the trolley at the checkout, group them together into categories. You could sort them into groups of frozen food, non-food household items, bottles and fragile things.

3. After the shopping has been scanned, pack the grouped items into the bags you've brought with you.

PACKING PERFECTION

★ Pack meat and frozen items together, to keep the meat cool.

★ Put all household and chemical items in a separate bag to the food, in case they leak.

★ Spread heavy items across the bottom of several bags – if using supermarket bags, use two bags, one inside the other for bottles.

★ Leave the fragile items, such as eggs and soft fruit, until last and fit them in around the tops of other bags to stop them from being crushed.

SKILL 54

CARE FOR A CACTUS

Cactuses are really cool house plants, and they're easy to take care of, too. Follow these DOs and DON'Ts to be a cactus king:

DO make sure your cactus has lots of sunlight. Place it on a sunny windowsill so it can soak up the sun.

DON'T get spiked! Your cactus will have some seriously sharp spines, so make sure you hold it by the pot, rather than the plant.

DO remember to water your cactus. Carefully test the soil with your finger, and if it feels completely dry, pour water over the soil in the pot from above.

DON'T over-water it. Cactuses need less water than other plants as they are used to desert conditions. Check the soil, and allow it to dry out completely before you water it, otherwise your cactus could suffer death by drowning!

SKILL 55

REMOVE STAINS

Don't let your coolest clothes get ruined by spills, splodges and splats. Find out how to get rid of stains:

STAIN: CHOCOLATE

★ Put the stained clothing in a plastic bag in the freezer until the chocolate has hardened, then scrape off the chocolate with a butter knife. Run the remaining stain under hot water and massage in a little washing up liquid. Wash the garment as normal (see **Skill 60**).

STAIN: INK

★ If the stain is on coloured fabric, soak it in a bowl of warm milk for a few minutes, then wash the garment as normal. If the stain is on white fabric, cover the stain with salt, then rub it with lemon juice and wash normally.

STAIN: GLUE

★ Ask your mum or sister for some nail varnish remover. Pour a small amount of it on to some cotton wool and dab away at the stain. Then put the garment in the washing machine as normal.

SKILL 56

TIDY YOUR BEDROOM IN FIVE MINUTES

Tidying up your room needn't take long – especially when you've got a million better things to do. You really only need five minutes, so start the clock:

1. Scoop up any dirty clothes and put them in the laundry basket. Put any clean clothes away in your wardrobe. See **Skill 74** for tips on folding clothes.

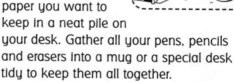

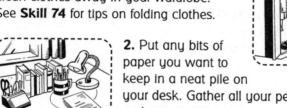

2. Put any bits of paper you want to keep in a neat pile on your desk. Gather all your pens, pencils and erasers into a mug or a special desk tidy to keep them all together.

3. Arrange books, DVDs and computer games in height order on your shelves.

4. Take any plates or mugs to the kitchen to wash up later (see **Skill 63**).

5. Make your bed. Plump up the pillow and put your PJs under it. Then shake out your duvet and smooth it down. Sit back and relax in your neat and tidy space.

SKILL 57

UNDO A JAMMED JAR LID

The next time you see someone struggling to open a pot of jam or marmalade, why not impress them by using brain power rather than brute strength? Here's how:

1. Run some hot water into a washing-up bowl. You want just enough to submerge the lid.

2. Carefully put the jar upside down in the water – make sure that the lid is submerged, but that the jar is not covered in water.

3. Wait for about a minute.

4. Carefully take out the jar and dry it with kitchen paper or a tea towel.

5. Dry your hands, too.

6. Twist the lid – you should find that it comes off easily.

7. If the lid is still stuck, put on rubber gloves to help you grip it better and try again.

SKILL 58

UNSTICK CHEWING GUM

If you've ever got a lump of gum on your clothes or shoes, you'll know what a sticky mess it can make. It's almost impossible to remove with your fingers, but a little bit of know-how makes all the difference:

1. Put the gummed-up garment or shoe in a plastic bag, then put it in the freezer. Leave it overnight if you can. If you can't wait that long, leave it for at least two hours.

2. Take the item out of the freezer. The chewing gum will have frozen solid. Carefully scrape away the gum with a butter knife.

3. If the item is too large to fit in your freezer, put some ice cubes into a plastic food bag and wrap an elastic band around the top to make sure the ice cubes stay put.

4. Place the bag of ice over the area of sticky gum and wait for it to harden. You can now remove the gum carefully with the butter knife.

5. Use a clean cloth soaked in warm, soapy water to dab at the area and get rid of any last bits of gum, then leave it to dry.

SKILL 59

HANG OUT THE WASHING

Giving your tumble dryer a break won't just save electricity, it can also help your clothes smell better and last longer. So, the next time the sun comes out, get pegging:

★ Ask an adult to help you to set up the washing line if it's not already up.

★ Shake out each item before you hang it on the line. This will minimize creases and wrinkles.

★ A bright, sunny day is great for drying your clothes, but it can make colours fade and whites go yellowish. Turn each item inside out to keep colours bright and whites white.

★ Hang shirts or T-shirts upside down and clip them to the line with pegs at both of the side seams.

★ Peg trousers by the legs, not the waist, so that the wind can get to them and blow them dry more easily.

★ When hanging out big sheets and bedding, fold them in half over the line then peg them at each end.

SKILL 60

DO THE LAUNDRY

Doing the washing is sure to make you really popular with your parents, so make sure you do it right by following these simple steps:

1. Sort all your laundry into different piles. Put all the white clothes in one pile. Sort through it carefully to make sure there are no dark socks lurking anywhere. Then make a pile of light-coloured clothes and a separate pile of dark-coloured clothes.

2. Go through all the pockets to check for coins (if you're lucky), which could damage the washing machine, or tissues (if you're less lucky), which could cover your clothing in fluffy white bits.

3. Look inside each item of clothing for the care label. This will give you the washing instructions you need. Look at the box below for help in understanding the most common symbols you will see.

CRACK THE LABEL CODE

40 60 =	Machine wash this garment at the temperature shown.
✋ =	Do not wash this in a washing machine. Hand wash it in cool water.
◯ =	Do not wash this in a washing machine. Take it to the dry cleaners.

4. Go through the colour piles and separate them into smaller groups of things that can be washed at the same temperature.

5. Put the first of these smaller groups of washing into the drum of the washing machine and close the door.

6. Most washing machines have a drawer at the top. Open the drawer and fill it with a scoop of washing powder, or a cap of liquid laundry detergent. Check the instructions on the packet to make sure you're using the right amount and putting it in the right place. Add a capful of fabric conditioner to the correct section of the drawer.

7. Choose a suitable setting on your washing machine for the type of wash you're doing. Every washing machine is different, so look closely at the buttons or dials on the front. Ask an adult to help you if you're still not sure.

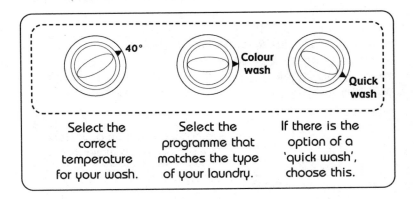

| Select the correct temperature for your wash. | Select the programme that matches the type of your laundry. | If there is the option of a 'quick wash', choose this. |

8. Press start, and leave the machine to finish its cycle. See **Skill 59** to find out how to hang your washing out to dry.

SKILL 61

USE UP THE ENDS OF PRODUCTS

Do the green thing and follow these tips to squeeze the last drop out of everything you use:

★ When things in bottles start to run out, store them upside down to get the very last drops and dribbles out of them.

★ Squeeze every bit out of tubes by curling them up tightly from the end. Use a clip or peg to secure the tube and keep it in position.

★ When tubes really are at the very end of their life, carefully snip the top off with a pair of scissors and you'll find that there is still some product left inside.

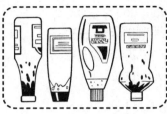

★ When batteries are running low, get more life out of them by taking them out of the product, rubbing them between your hands, then re-inserting them.

SKILL 62

PACK A SUITCASE

Do you find packing for a holiday or school trip a real pain? Follow these steps for some superbly simple suitcase packing:

1. Think about where you're going, how long you're staying and what you're going to be doing there – will you need any special equipment?

2. Make a list of everything you want to take with you, then lay everything out near your suitcase.

3. Fold bulky items such as jeans and trousers in half, and put these at the bottom of your case. Fold tops and shirts and layer them on top of the trousers.

4. Roll up pants and socks then put them inside your shoes. These can go around the edges with the soles facing out.

5. Put anything liquid or breakable in a plastic bag. Put this in the middle of the suitcase, cushioned by the clothes for safety.

SKILL SUGGESTION

Going on a plane? Your case will go in the hold, so take a smaller bag on the plane with a toothbrush and some clean underwear in it, in case your case goes missing.

DO THE WASHING-UP

When you've run out of excuses and it's time to do the washing-up, here's how to make it simple:

1. Turn on the taps and half fill the sink or bowl with hot water. Add two or three squirts of washing-up liquid as you run the water.

> **SKILL SUGGESTION**
>
> Soak dirty pans in soapy water to loosen dried-on food before you wash them up.

2. Wear rubber gloves and test the water with your finger, so you don't scald yourself.

3. Place all the things you're washing up near the sink. Tackle the things that have touched your mouth first – they will need the hottest water. This means washing glasses and cups first, then the cutlery, then plates and bowls and finally, pans.

4. Submerge each item you're washing in the bowl or sink then use a washing-up sponge or cloth to rub it clean. Rinse it with clean water for a few seconds so the soapy water runs off.

5. Stack clean items on a draining rack. Use a container to stack cutlery upright.

6. Change the water if it gets too dirty or cold.

SKILL 64

CLEAN WINDOWS

Earn yourself a pocket money raise by making the windows sparkling clean:

WARNING

Never clean outside windows that are higher than the ground floor. Leave these to an adult.

1. Start with the outside windows. Half fill a bucket with warm water and add a small squirt of washing-up liquid to it.

2. Put on rubber gloves. Dip a sponge into the bucket, then squeeze it out to get rid of the excess water.

3. Wipe the sponge over the glass of the window, using sideways motions.

4. Use a cleaning tool called a squeegee to get rid of excess water. Then dry the glass with a chamois leather or soft cloth – rub it in circular movements over the glass to make it shine.

5. Repeat **steps 2** to **4** on the inside windows. Lay down old newspaper first to protect the floor from drips.

SKILL SUGGESTION

Clean windows on a cloudy day. The sun can make the glass dry too quickly and leave streaks behind.

SKILL 65

CLEAR A TABLE

Show how much you enjoyed a tasty dinner by offering to clear the table. Here is what to do:

1. Wait until everyone has finished their meal before clearing up – no one likes having their plate taken away mid-mouthful! If you're not sure whether or not someone has finished, just ask.

2. Clear one plate at a time. Stand to one side of the diner and don't reach over. If you do, you could spill something on their lap – splat!

3. As you get more confident, take two or more plates stacked on top of each other, keeping all the cutlery together on the top plate – but don't overdo it. Take the plates into the kitchen and scrape off any unfinished food into a bin.

4. Tackle glasses and cups or mugs next. Carry one mug in each hand by its handle or one glass in each hand by its bottom, and take them into the kitchen where you can pour any leftovers down the sink. Then use a damp cloth to wipe the table and tablemats clean, or shake out the tablecloth outside.

SKILL 66

DUST LIKE A PRO

Dispose of dust in no time with these simple steps:

1. Dust tends to fall downwards when disturbed, so make sure you start at the top shelf or highest point in the room first. This way, you won't accidentally re-cover clean areas with dust.

2. Take anything you can carry – such as rugs and cushions – outside and beat them in the open air to banish dust. Use a tennis racket if you really want to beat away the dust.

3. Don't dust around objects – this leaves a tell-tale trail. Instead, be thorough and lift every item off tables and shelves. Dust the item then the surface underneath it before carefully putting the item back.

4. Use a clean, soft dusting cloth and make slow movements with it over the area you are dusting. The aim is to catch the dust in the cloth – not swirl it up into the air, so take it slowly and carefully.

5. Don't let the duster get overloaded. Open a window or door and shake the dust out of the cloth every few minutes.

SORT THE RECYCLING

Recycling is a great way to do your bit for the environment and reduce waste. Develop good habits by following the guide below:

BEFORE YOU START

Make sure you know what you can recycle – check your local council's website if you're not sure.

1. To make helping the planet a breeze for you and your family, set up a recycling point at home. Use a large box (some councils provide these – ask an adult to check whether your house will get one or not) and place it near your kitchen bin.

2. To make sure that everyone in your house knows what can and what can't be recycled, attach a list of recyclable items to the side of the box with sticky tape.

3. Find out from an adult what day the recycling is collected and make sure you place the box outside – by your front door or at the kerbside – before the collection time.

Some recyclables need special preparation before they go in the box. Read on to find out more.

GLASS

★ Carefully rinse out any bottles or jars that have had food or drink in them. Dry them thoroughly and place them gently in the recycling box.

★ Always wear rubber gloves when dealing with glass, to protect your hands in case it shatters.

★ Most lids and caps are made of different, non-recyclable materials, so separate these and put them in your bin.

METAL

★ Wash out any tins or cans that have had food or drink in them. Be careful as the edges may be sharp.

★ Crush cans down to use as little space as possible in the recycling box. Make sure the cans are completely empty before you do this.

PAPER AND CARDBOARD

★ Break down and flatten cereal packets and other cardboard boxes to take up less space.

★ Any paper or cardboard that has food residue or greasy stuff on it will not be recyclable. Tear or cut these bits off and put them in your waste bin, then place the clean parts in the recycling container.

SKILL 68

LOAD A DISHWASHER

Did you know, there is an art to loading a dishwasher, which means you get everything cleaner more quickly? Here's how:

THE BOTTOM

1. Load the bottom of the dishwasher first.

2. Rinse off large chunks of food and place plates in the grooves that fit them.

3. Load cutlery into the basket, with the blades of knives pointing down.

4. Make sure the washing arm under the top rack can spin freely.

THE TOP

5. Put all glasses and cups upside down on the top layer. Make sure that tall glasses fit before you close the door.

6. Make sure smaller items won't get washed off the top layer and on to the bottom of the machine.

DON'T put anything plastic, such as beakers, at the bottom of the dishwasher as they might melt.

DO save water by only running the dishwasher when it is full.

DON'T put large, sharp knives in the dishwasher as it's best to wash these (carefully) by hand. See **Skill 63** for some top washing-up tips.

DON'T put in silverware or anything else that isn't marked 'dishwasher safe', such as crystal or expensive dinner plates. Ask an adult if you're not sure.

DO wait for the dishwasher to finish. Stand back when opening the door, as there will be a cloud of hot steam that could scald you.

DO unload the bottom level first as water may drip from items above.

SKILL 69

PUT ON A DUVET COVER

Putting on a duvet cover doesn't have to be a wrestling match. Turn yourself into a duvet master with this easy-to-follow guide:

1. Flatten out your duvet on the bed, then turn your clean duvet cover inside out and lay it flat over the duvet, making sure the fastenings are undone.

2. Put your arms inside the cover until you reach the corners of the duvet cover that are furthest away.

3. Grab the top corners of the duvet while keeping your hands inside the cover, then shake the cover down over it, so the cover is now the right way out.

4. Push the other two corners of the duvet into the bottom corners of the duvet cover.

5. Close the fastenings and give the duvet a final big shake or two, before smoothing it over your bed.

SKILL 70

VACUUM YOUR BEDROOM

Here's a tried and trusted way to put a smile on your parents' faces – clean your bedroom floor:

1. Clear books and clothes off the floor. Tidy away what you can, and put the rest on your bed.

2. Place the vacuum cleaner in the middle of your bedroom and plug it in. Let out lots of cord, so that you can move freely about the room without tugging the plug out of the socket.

3. Turn the vacuum cleaner on and turn it up to maximum power. Place the wide brush flat, so the bristles are touching the floor.

4. Push the brush over the surface of your floor, making backwards and forwards sweeping motions. Make sure you clean under your desk, chair and bed.

5. Turn the vacuum cleaner off and change the brush for the small, pointed 'crevice nozzle' (shown here), so you can clean the corners, nooks and edges of the room.

6. Switch off the vacuum cleaner when you're done, unplug it and tidy up the cord.

FOLD A BIG SHEET

Grab a friend, or ask your mum, dad, brother or sister to give you a hand, then follow these steps for some super-fast sheet folding:

1. Open out the sheet to its full size and lay it out flat on the bed, or on a large table.

2. Hold the sheet by its bottom two corners and ask your helper to hold the corners at the top.

3. Lift the sheet and walk a few steps away from each other, so that it stretches taut.

The next steps are meant for both you and your helper. Give him or her a nod or say, 'Go!' before you do each one to make sure you both fold at the same time.

4. Bring your hands together so that the corners you are holding touch and the sheet is folded in half lengthways.

5. Keep holding the corners together with one hand, but take your right hand off the sheet and ask your helper to take his or her left hand off.

6. Reach down with your free hand and grab the bottom corner of the sheet and ask your helper to do the same. Pull it so the sheet is taut, then bring this hand up level with the other.

7. Holding the corners, walk towards each other until you're standing close together and the sheet is hanging in a 'U' shape. Ask your helper to grab the top corners of the sheet while you reach down to pick up the bottom corners.

8. Walk back again to stretch the folded sheet out and repeat **steps 4** to **8** until the sheet is folded neatly.

SKILL 72

RAKE UP LEAVES

If your garden is in danger of disappearing under a carpet of autumn leaves, impress your parents with this super-efficient way to rake them up:

1. Wrap up in long sleeves, gloves and sturdy jeans to protect you from thorns.

2. Choose a day that is dry with only a light breeze.

3. Using a strong, wide rake, reach out into the leaves as far as you can, put the tines (prongs) of the rake on the ground then drag it back towards you. Make small piles of leaves as you go.

4. Place an old sheet flat on the ground beside the pile, then use sweeping strokes of the rake to move the leaves on to it.

5. Pull up all four corners of the sheet, so the leaves are safely bundled inside. Carry them over to your compost bin or garden recycling container and shake the leaves out into it.

6. Keep going until you have swept the ground clear.

SKILL SUGGESTION

If you don't have a compost bin, shake the leaves into bin liners and tie them at the top. Ask an adult to check if your leaves can be collected by the council.

SKILL 73

MOP A FLOOR

Here's how to turn yourself into a mopping maestro:

1. Before you get mopping, vacuum the floor to get rid of any dust and grime on the surface.

2. Put on rubber gloves and half-fill a bucket with warm water. Add a small amount of floor cleaner. Read the instructions on the packaging to find out how much to add.

3. Dip the mop in the bucket. If your mop has a lever on it, pull this now to squeeze out the excess water from the mop. If it doesn't, wring out the mop into the bucket with your hands.

4. If your mop has a sponge head, move it in a sweeping motion straight up and down on the floor. If your mop has a rag head, swirl it around the floor in a figure-of-eight motion.

5. Start at one end of the room and work backwards, so you don't step on the floor you've already cleaned. Keep dipping the mop in the bucket and wringing it out as you go.

6. Make sure you change the water in the bucket if it gets too dirty, and don't walk on the floor until it's dry.

SKILL 74

PUT YOUR CLOTHES AWAY

Follow these top folding tips to make sure you always look smart and ready for anything:

TIP-TOP TOPS AND T-SHIRTS

1. Turn T-shirts, polo shirts and jumpers over so they are face down on a flat surface.

2. Take one sleeve and fold it over from the shoulder seam so that the sleeve is pointing downwards and is in the middle of the back of the T-shirt, as shown.

3. Repeat **step 2** with the other sleeve.

4. Pick up the top and fold it in half, with the sleeves on the inside, so it's roughly rectangular, then place it in a drawer.

BE A JEANS GENIUS

1. Flatten out jeans and other trousers and lay them out on a flat surface. Fold them in half lengthways with one leg on top of the other, as shown here.

2. Fold the jeans or trousers in half widthways and hang them over a coat hanger in your wardrobe.

GET SHIRT SMART

1. Hang clean shirts on coat hangers, using one shirt per hanger, and smooth them down to make sure there are no wrinkles.

2. Do up one or two buttons to keep them on the hanger. Hang the hangers in your wardrobe.

SOCK IT TO THEM

1. Sort through clean socks and find all the matching pairs.

2. Take a matching pair, hold the tops of the socks together, and roll them over into each other, forming a ball that will keep them together.

3. Keep all your paired up socks together in a drawer.

EMERGENCY SKILLS

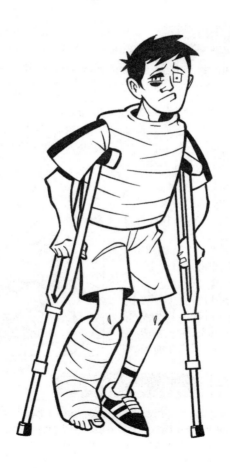

SKILL 75

REMOVE A SPLINTER

Getting a splinter of wood stuck under your skin is not only annoying – it also hurts. Follow these steps to remove splinters simply and painlessly:

1. Use a magnifying glass or mirror to inspect the splinter and see exactly where it is.

2. Wash your hands, then wash the area around the splinter and dry it carefully by dabbing it with paper towels.

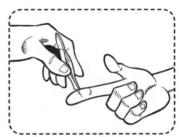

3. Use a clean pair of tweezers to ease the splinter out. Do this by pressing down just underneath the point it's poking out from. Grab the splinter between the tips of the tweezers and slowly pull it out in the opposite direction to which it went in.

4. After the splinter is out, put the area under running water to wash away any blood or tiny splinters. Dry it and put a blob of antiseptic cream on it.

SKILL SUGGESTION

If you can't get the splinter out, have a hot bath or shower. The steam will open your pores, and make it easier to remove the splinter.

SKILL 76

TREAT A BURN

If you or one of your friends gets burned or scalded, then you need to keep calm and act fast. Here's what to do:

1. Assess the injury. If the burn is bigger than a postage stamp, is deep, or is around the mouth or throat, call 999 immediately (see **Skill 77**). If it is a minor burn then you can treat it yourself.

WARNING

Never use fizzy drinks, ice cubes or ointments on the burnt area.

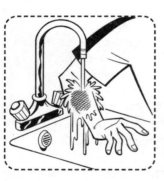

2. Run cool water over the burnt area of skin for at least 15 minutes. If you can't reach running water you can submerge the burn in milk, cold juice or tepid water.

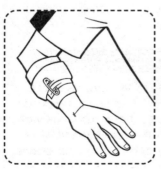

3. Once the area has cooled down, place a non-fluffy bandage loosely over the wound and secure it with a safety pin. If you don't have a bandage, use a clean plastic bag for an injured hand or use a clean piece of plastic wrap for scalded arms or legs. Don't wrap it too tightly, in case the burn swells up.

SKILL 77

CALL THE EMERGENCY SERVICES

If you're ever in the position of having to dial 999, it's important to know what to do to make sure help gets to you as quickly as possible. Here are some useful tips:

1. Decide if you need to ring 999. You should only call if there is a fire, if someone's life is in danger, or if a serious crime is taking place. Make sure you get yourself to a safe place before you make the call.

2. Don't panic. You will be asked several questions and your answers could save lives. Speak clearly and give as much information as possible. Take deep breaths to help keep calm.

3. Tell the person you speak to whether you need the fire service, ambulance or police. Give your own name and the phone number you are calling from, so that they can call you back.

4. Say where the emergency is happening. If you don't know the exact address, try to give a street name or a landmark that you can see, such as a shop or a restaurant.

5. Always follow the advice you are given by the trained operator, and wait for the ambulance, fire engine or police car to arrive.

SKILL SUGGESTION

Calls to 999 are free from mobiles, land lines and phone boxes, so you can always make the call, even if you have no money or credit on your phone.

☆

SKILL 78

TREAT A BEE STING

Getting stung can really put a downer on a day in the sunshine. Here's how to deal with a sting:

1. Remove the sting using the edge of a nail, a bank card or even the edge of a ruler. To do this, scrape it across the sting in a scooping motion.

2. Wash around the wound with soap and water. The area around the sting may be swollen and throbbing. Don't worry, this is normal. Put ice cubes or a bag of frozen peas over the area to cool it.

3. Ask an adult for some soothing cream and rub it into your skin. Wrap the area in a cold flannel and, if you've been stung on your arm or leg, raise it up to reduce swelling.

4. If you develop a rash, feel dizzy or can't breathe properly, or if your tongue, eyes or lips swell up, get help immediately.

SKILL 79

TIE A SLING

If a friend has hurt his arm, you can give it support and help ease the pain by making and tying a sling. Here's how:

1. Take a large square of fabric and fold it in half to make a triangle.

2. Ask the patient to hold his injured arm across his chest, bent at the elbow.

3. Put the triangle underneath the injured arm, with the longest side of the triangle towards his fingers and the top end up over his shoulder and around the back of his neck.

4. Gently pull the bottom of the fabric up over the arm to support it. Bring this end up to meet the other end at the shoulder.

5. Tie the ends of the sling together around the back of the patient's neck. Check that the sling is not too tight. You should be able to see the patient's fingers poking out.

6. Fold the loose fabric at the elbow over and secure it carefully with a safety pin, as shown here.

☆

SKILL 80

STOP SOMEONE CHOKING

If a friend starts choking on a piece of food, you need to act fast. Here's what to do:

1. Tell him to cough – this may be enough to clear the blockage.

2. If your friend can't clear his throat by coughing, stand behind him. Explain that you are going to try to clear the blockage by sharply tapping him on the back five times.

3. Gently lean your friend forwards then give him five short, sharp whacks on the back with the heel of your hand. Check if the blockage has cleared after each whack. Repeat if necessary.

4. If you still can't clear the blockage, tell your friend to stay calm, while you dial 999 (see **Skill 77**).

WARNING

If the person choking cannot speak or breathe, do not attempt to deal with it yourself. Fetch an adult and call 999 immediately.

SKILL 81

DRESS A CUT

Unless you wrap yourself in bubble wrap, cuts and scrapes are going to happen. Here's how to treat them, so they heal quickly:

WARNING

If the cut is deep, or is longer than 1 cm, tell an adult and seek medical attention, rather than trying to dress it yourself. It may need stitches, which can only be done by a medical professional.

---

1. Wash and dry your hands thoroughly to minimize the risk of infection.

2. Put the cut area under lukewarm running water. This helps clean the injury. If you see gravel, splinters or pieces of glass caught in the wound, ask an adult for help.

3. If the cut is still bleeding, apply direct pressure to it with a clean cloth to slow the flow of blood.

4. Use a clean piece of fabric to pat the area around the cut dry. Don't use anything fluffy that might leave material in the cut.

5. Gently put some antiseptic cream on the cut and the skin around it.

6. Place a plaster or a non-fluffy bandage tightly over the cut, making sure that it's completely covered.

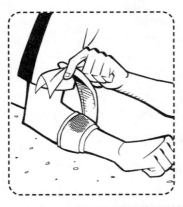

7. If blood seeps through the first dressing you have applied, place another one over the top of it.

WARNING

If blood seeps through the second dressing too, remove both and reapply fresh ones. It's important that you then seek medical attention, to see if you need stitches to help the cut heal.

SKILL 82

PUT SOMEONE IN THE RECOVERY POSITION

If someone is unconscious, putting them in the recovery position will ensure they can breathe while you wait for an ambulance. Practise the steps below with a friend, so you know what to do:

WARNING

The recovery position is the best way of keeping a casualty safe until medical help arrives.

However, if you think the person may have hurt their spine, by falling for example, moving them could make their injuries worse. If you are in this situation, then wait for the ambulance to arrive and talk to the paramedics.

1. Kneel down next to the casualty and move the arm nearest you into an 'L' shape with the back of the hand on the ground.

2. Put your palm in his other hand. Move his hand up so the back of it is against his face. Don't remove your hand.

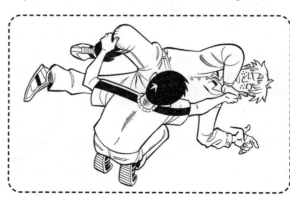

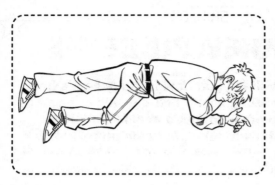

3. Pull the casualty's furthest knee up, so that his foot is flat on the floor. Keep your hand on his knee and roll him gently towards you, and on to his side, as shown.

4. Carefully remove your hand from under the casualty's head, and gently tilt his head back slightly to make sure he can breathe.

5. Remain calm and stay with the casualty until the ambulance arrives. Tell the paramedics what has happened.

> **WARNING**
>
> If you're doing this for real, not just practising with a friend, make sure you dial 999 before beginning to move the casualty (see **Skill 77**).

SKILL 83

TAKE A PULSE

Taking a pulse will tell you how fast a person's heart is beating. It's a really useful first-aid skill to have, as it will tell you more about a person's injuries. Here's how to take your own pulse:

1. Hold out one hand, with your palm facing up, and keeping your arm relaxed.

2. Put your index and middle finger on the inside of the wrist, near the thumb and just below the crease where the hand meets the arm. You will feel your pulse in 'beats'. These beats are actually the blood moving underneath your skin.

3. When you've found your pulse, keep constant pressure on the spot with your fingers, and count the number of beats you feel in ten seconds. Multiply the number you get by six to work out how many beats your pulse makes in a minute.

SKILL SUGGESTION

If you can't find a pulse at the wrist, put your index and middle fingers on the side of the neck below the jawline.

Did You Know? A resting heart rate (your heart rate when you have just woken up in the morning) can be anything between 60 and 100 beats per minute for children. If your pulse rate worries you, tell an adult.

SKILL 84

BE SAFE IN A FIRE

If you're ever caught in a fire, follow these steps to keep yourself out of danger:

1. As with any emergency, stay calm. If you panic, you are more likely to do something reckless, which may put you in danger.

2. Get out of the building. Walk quickly, but don't run as you could trip over. Don't take anything with you – it's more important to save yourself than your favourite computer game! Don't use lifts on your way out, as the fire may have made them unsafe.

3. Fires can be tricky and unpredictable. When you're moving to get outside, feel any doors with the palm of your hand before you open them. If the door or handle feels warm, there could be a fire on the other side of it, so take an alternative route to safety.

4. Keep low. Fires produce lots of smoke, which can make it difficult for you to breathe. The air is clearer near the floor, so crouch down as you move, or crawl on your hands and knees. Cover your mouth and nose with a wet cloth to help you breathe.

5. Call 999 as soon as you are out of the building (see **Skill 77**) Never go back into a building until the fire service has told you it is safe to do so.

SKILL 85
STOP A NOSEBLEED
Follow these simple steps to deal with nasty nosebleeds:

1. Find somewhere comfortable to sit down.

2. Position a bucket on the floor just in front of you and lean forwards slightly so your nose is directly above the bucket.

3. Squeeze the softest part of your nose (between the end and the bony ridge) with your thumb and index finger. Breathe through your mouth.

4. Keep squeezing here for at least 10 to 15 minutes or until you feel the bleeding has stopped.

Don't blow your nose afterwards, as this may start the bleeding again.

WARNING

Go to see a doctor if ...

★ ... your nosebleed was caused by a fall or injury.

★ ... you get nosebleeds very often.

★ ... your nose continues to bleed heavily for more than 30 minutes.

☆

SKILL 86
DEAL WITH CRAMP

Muscle cramps can take you by surprise and they don't half hurt! Here's how to get rid of them:

1. Stop what you are doing – trying to continue moving or exercising will make the cramp worse.

2. Gently massage the cramping muscle with your fingers. If the cramp is in your foot, gently flex your foot up towards your shin to stretch the muscles.

3. Apply ice to the sore muscle. This will help get your circulation going and will ease the cramp.

TACKLE CALF CRAMP

★ Cramps commonly affect the calf muscles in your legs, and can sometimes happen while you're asleep.

★ To prevent calf cramp, before you exercise, stretch your calf muscles by placing the palms of your hands flat against a wall. Move one leg backwards and straighten it, so your heel is flat on the floor. Bend the knee of your other leg, and lean into the wall as shown. Hold the stretch for 20 seconds, then swap legs.